The First Peace Circle

A Guide
To Creating a
First Peace Circle

Second Edition

WindEagle and RainbowHawk

World Foundation for the Discipline of Peace
A Global Expression of Ehama Institute

*Dear Ellen,
Your spirit feels deep & powerful. Many Blessing on your way.
WindEagle*

*Dear Ellen
It is a Joy to have had this time together!
Blessing to you
RainbowHawk*

Printed in the United States of America
Second Printing December 2009
ISBN:1440419957

First Peace Logo - Silk Painting by Alowan Linton

Photos from Dreamstime.com

World Foundation for the Discipline of Peace
A Global Expression of Ehama Institute
Email: firstpeace@disciplineofpeace.org
Visit our website at: www.disciplineofpeace.org
Visit our First Peace Community site at: http://firstpeace.ning.com

Booklet Design and Layout: FireHawk - www.resonance.to

"The First Peace, which is the most important, is that which comes within the souls of people when they realize their relationship, their oneness, with the Universe and all its powers, and when they realize that at the center of the Universe dwells Wakan Tanka, the Great Spirit, and that this center is everywhere, and it is within each of us. This is the real peace, and others are but reflections of this.

The second peace is that which is made by two individuals, and the third is that which is made between two nations.

But above all you should understand that there can never be peace between nations until there is known that true peace, which, as I have often said, is within the souls of the people."

Black Elk – Oglala Sioux Spiritual Leader 18th Century

1

THE EIGHT UNIVERSAL
PRINCIPLES OF PEACE

Introduction

In order to create the world we long for, it is imperative to find new ways - of coming together, of listening more deeply, of finding solutions and of thinking and perceiving.

All of humanity is being called to attention by our earth planet and an evolving state of consciousness that is shifting our collective awareness. It is the purpose of this handbook to assist in the evolution of human consciousness toward peace on earth.

We, each of us, have the capacity to make the state of peace a reality now, a reality that touches every part of our world, and becomes stronger and stronger as it spreads as a culture to all lands.

To awaken this capacity, we must together explore the nature of this state we call peace. What conditions allow it to grow and thrive? What conditions cause this state to diminish and be forgotten?

The words of Black Elk, an Oglala Sioux spiritual leader in the 18th century, which are quoted in the forepart of this handbook, make clear where we humans must begin: "in the realization and consciousness within each individual".

This realization and consciousness of peace starts here, in each one of us. Like a seedling, this realization of peace and consciousness grows and influences all life around us and becomes a first movement that combines and amplifies with the first movements of other humans (or individuals) to become a culture in which all of humanity resides. In registering as a First Peace Circle in joining this people's movement, each member of the circle will be contributing to creating this culture of consciousness in the world.

There are many movements toward creating a consciousness of peace in the world, and the World Foundation for the Discipline of Peace is but one of them. First Peace Circles have unique elements to contribute to these movements toward making peace a reality now. That is the purpose of this handbook, to contribute to how we can work together in this exploration and implementation.

Let's create the First Peace together, now.

Understanding the Evolving Nature of the Universe

The process of human understanding of our Universe has been a long story of our collective yearning as humans to probe the mystery of who we are and our quest to give meaning to life.

Most recently the ways of scientific study have lead to quantum physics and its postulations on how the Universe works and evolves. Interestingly, there are many correlations between what modern physics is revealing and what ancient earth cultures have held as the nature of the Universe over thousands of years.

Prominent among these ancient earth cultures are the Mayan and pre-Mayan peoples, who evolved a sophisticated understanding of the Universe called The Sacred Twenty Count. This understanding of the Universe was held in a circular design with all the various energies of the Universe flowing from it. The circular design starts as number one, Sun, and proceeds to the number twenty, Great Spirit. The whole count includes the numbers from one to twenty and includes everything in the Universe, the seen and the unseen.

All creation stories that come from this culture have an evolving theme that leads to various stages of worlds that have a similarity to the epochs that modern science holds as the history of evolution. It is from these ancient teachings and the correlations modern science has revealed that the Eight Universal Principles are derived.

The Eight Universal Principles are the foundation for the consciousness of the First Peace.

I am awakening	E	Spirit as light emanates life force
	SE	True presence is the doorway to the Great Mystery
	S	Wholeness is only experienced through diversity
I am remembering	SW	The essence of identity is embedded in cellular memory
I am honoring	W	The darkness in the holy womb of life contains all light
I am dreaming	NW	The universal relationship of co-creation exists through cause and effect
I am walking	N	Universal truth informs right action
I am tending guarding	NE	All things are born of woman

8,18 NW
bluish-purple lavender

4,14 blue
N animals

9,19 green
moons

purple   2,12   W ———⊗——— 5,10,15,20 ——— E 1,11 yellow light

magenta reddish purple 7,17   SW

S
3,13
red plants

SE 6,16
orange ancestry

5

Spirit As Light
Emanates Life Force

6

True Presence is
the Doorway to
the Great Mystery

7

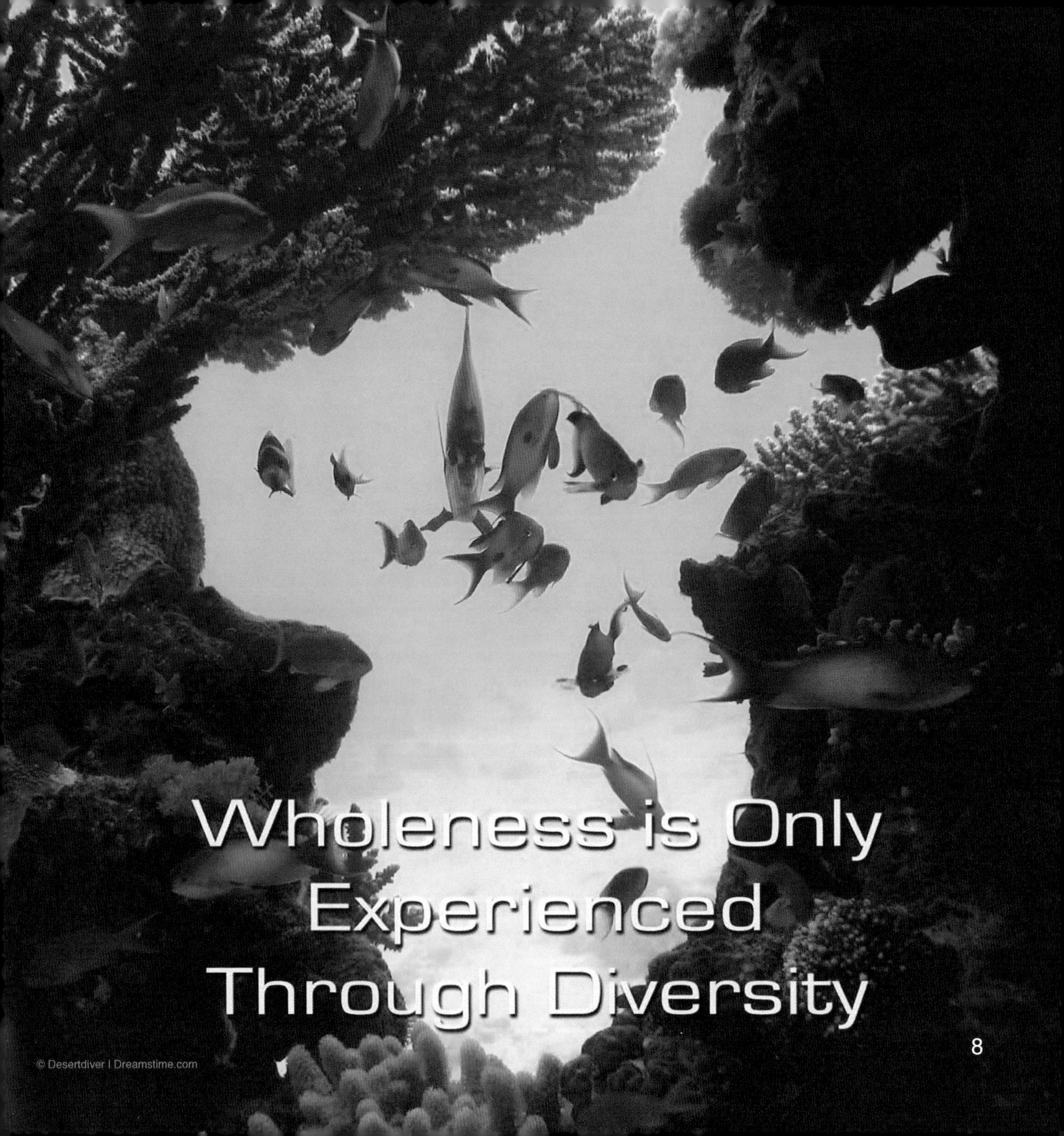

Wholeness is Only
Experienced
Through Diversity
© Desertdiver | Dreamstime.com

The Essence of Identity
is Embedded
in Cellular Memory

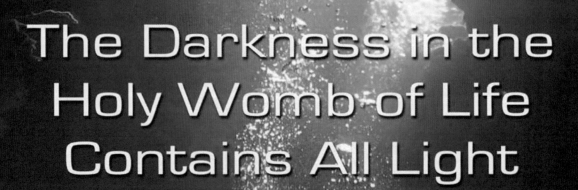

The Darkness in the
Holy Womb of Life
Contains All Light

10

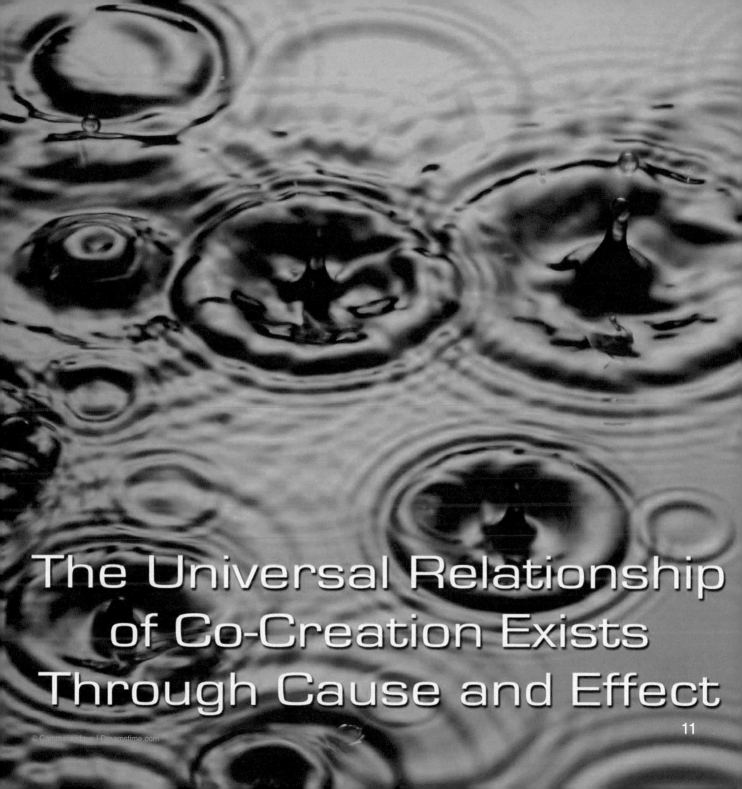

The Universal Relationship
of Co-Creation Exists
Through Cause and Effect

11

Universal Truth
Informs Right Action

All Things Are
Born of Woman

The First Peace

We welcome you, as together we grow and develop the First Peace. This reference to the First Peace comes from a quote from Black Elk, Oglala Sioux, in which he states "The First Peace is that which comes from within the souls of people when they realize their relationship, their oneness, with the Universe and all its powers...."

Realizing our oneness with the Universe is at the heart of the vision of the Discipline of Peace. When we open our understanding to this truth, peace in the self becomes a reality. This living of peace in the self is a vital step for all of us, for each of us.

In this time in which we live, we see the very necessary and vital need for humanity to take another step toward creating not only peace in each of us, but peace among us. Collaborating with each other, learning from each other and celebrating our many wisdom ways are essential parts of the vision of the First Peace Circles.

First Peace Circles

First Peace Circles are meant to inspire deep and evocative exploration through the study and practice of universal peace principles among small groups of people who are interested in the many different ways we can live peace in the self.

The Principles and Practices in this handbook are offered as the first seeds to plant and foster, with the understanding that through a Circle's exploration and each person's own practice, there will be many more seeds that grow in each garden of consciousness.

The vision is that these First Peace Circles and the seeds of practice will grow and spread like a wave of higher consciousness lifting us all to a new level for all humanity.

Living the First Peace

Calling the First Peace awake in us is all about practice.

Circles are akin to the water, sun and minerals and we each are the soil.

To make change in the self requires a practice - one we live each day.

The practice of peace calls for us to plant the seeds of peace in the garden of ourselves and to foster their growth, daily.

The purpose of the First Peace Circles is to open and stimulate exploration of the wonder of the Universe and to support each other in the practice of Living Peace.

Pay It Forward

Young people, all over the world, are the stewards of the collective consciousness on this planet.

Working in concert, we can create a 'tipping point' towards creating peace on our planet.

Some young people are already active and sharing deeply and profoundly the wisdom they carry.

One of the aims of the First Peace Circles is for each participant to share the understanding they have in themselves of the First Peace with at least one young person.

PRACTICES FOR EACH PRINCIPLE

Image from Hubbell Space Telescope

SPIRIT, AS LIGHT, EMANATES LIFE FORCE
There is no restraint or boundary to the evolving
of the spirit's manifestation.

PRAYER DANCE OF AWAKENING
Awaken each day to your
prayer thought of your I AM.

Express this prayer thought through sound,
movement and visualization.

Set this as a ground of consciousness
throughout each day's experience.

Practice for Principle #1
PRAYER DANCE OF AWAKENING

There is no restraint or boundary to the evolving of the spirit's manifestation.

With this universal principle is the call to realize that as humans we are a manifestation of light in human form, a manifestation of the Divine, and as such we are called to develop this consciousness that has no restraint or boundary.

The practice that is offered, Prayer Dance of Awakening, is coming deeply into the consciousness of the spirit that we are, connecting to the truth of our being and recognizing fully that we are intimately related to the powers of the Universe, the Deity, which is everywhere, and in each human.

When in relationship with this truth, we can allow this knowing to flow into the I AM consciousness (our spirit consciousness) and grow our ever-expanding awareness of this state.

The purpose of this practice is to make this realization the ground of our being from which our experience can emerge.

To continue to develop this consciousness, it is necessary to allow the I AM to be the foundational thought of all our thoughts, and to let this consciousness grow and evolve as the fundamental truth of who we are. This truth is intimately related to the powers of the Universe, the Deity, which is everywhere.

The practice of being this I AM is to do the Prayer Dance of Awakening, beginning each day in the morning, and allow that awakened energy to flow into and through all the activities of our day.

To do this, allow the I AM thought to be expressed in the body's movement of energy, combined with sound expression and images and thoughts. Develop and evolve your own powerful way of awakening this higher consciousness, with your own images.

To allow this power of thought of higher consciousness to form and root in us is an honoring of the truth of our true spirit self.

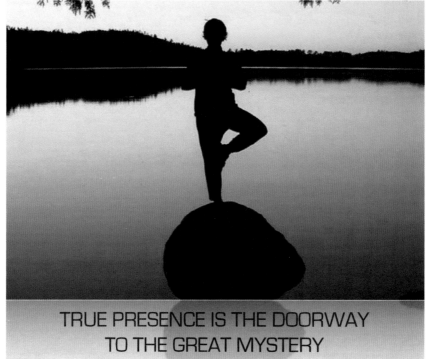

TRUE PRESENCE IS THE DOORWAY
TO THE GREAT MYSTERY
The awakening of presence in each moment is
an open gateway to the unity of all creation.

OPENING THE GATEWAY
During experiences of your day,
step into a heightened state
of sensate awareness.
Become still.
Open to the depth of presence.

Incorporate a daily practice time for
meditation, contemplation and deep listening.

Practice for Principle #2
OPENING THE GATEWAY

The awakening of presence in each moment is an open gateway to the unity of all creation.

In becoming aware of deep presence we use a phrase from an eastern tradition: "not two". This expression is a teaching that we are not separate from the Universe and the spirit in all things. When we can awaken ourselves to this state of being, we realize we are united with all creation.

In opening this second practice called Opening the Gateway, it is important to realize that to be truly present in the moment that is being experienced, the thinking mind must be stilled.

At the same time, the level of heightened sensate awareness of the moment must be engaged in a form of deep receptivity called "stillness".

This state of stillness, when it is connected with the I Am state of consciousness, can help us be open to the energies of the Universe. We can then be open to the Universe to receive messages and information to the various levels of our consciousness.

To develop this second practice, we need TO BE "stillness" which is entering the realm where creation is constantly occurring, which is in connection with source. Practice of this state can be experienced through meditation, contemplation and deep listening.

Practice the state of stillness at different times and in the varied circumstances of your day. For example, when walking down a busy street or when faced with a challenge.

This practice, when deepened will allow you to drop into stillness, at moments when you feel under pressure and access your I AM consciousness.

© Desertdiver I Dreamstime.com

WHOLENESS IS ONLY EXPERIENCED THROUGH DIVERSITY

The evolution of the spirit is fostered
by the state of openness and trust.

TRANSCENDING EGO
The natural state of the I AM is
to be in openness and trust.
The moment you become aware
of any diminishment of
the state of openness and trust,
step into stillness.
Remember the truth of the I AM
and step into the life affirming
power of response.

Practice for Principle #3
TRANSCENDING EGO

The evolution of the spirit is fostered by the state of openness and trust.

To begin it is important to realize that our natural state is one of openness and trust. By this it is meant that our trust and openness is part of the health of our being and is based on trust for the self. The experience of this kind of trust supports our ability to be open to what comes our way knowing that we will meet it and respond in a way that is life affirming.

When we contemplate the third Universal Principle, "Wholeness is Only Experienced through Diversity", we need to understand that the Universe, in evolving the manifestation of life in all its forms, has made diversity manifest in everything. For instance, all tree life in every species is unique and every tree is different. Of course, each one is a part of the whole and each unique species is what makes the wholeness.

Because this uniqueness is in all things, we must be able to experience this diversity of manifestation to see what is present in our life and to be open to perceive difference or diversity.   When we can be open, even appreciative toward the differences we experience, we can begin to live this principle.

By being open and appreciative we are meeting the experience from a place of understanding.   In order to understand and appropriately respond, we need to see deeply into what we are experiencing from the consciousness of the I AM. The I AM is naturally in a state of openness and trust.

However, the ego disconnected from the I AM, not guided by it, is often thrust into distrust when encountering diversity, or something it is not comfortable with.

In developing this higher consciousness, the practice of Transcending Ego is to develop a heightened alertness to when we experience a feeling of closing or becoming defensive and shifting to trusting ourselves to see into and respond appropriately to what is confronting us. Use this to practice the state of openness. Observe when we tend to close and what is affecting us.   Observe any conditions that support our openness and trust.

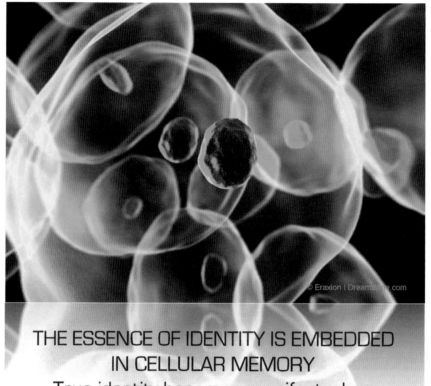

THE ESSENCE OF IDENTITY IS EMBEDDED IN CELLULAR MEMORY

True identity becomes manifest when
consciousness remembers its divine nature.

REMEMBERING SACRED PATH

During your day's activities, give
yourself times of spaciousness
when you stop to remember
the spirit of the I AM to help
you recall your true purpose and
to reorient to your sacred path.

Practice for Principle #4
REMEMBERING SACRED PATH

True identity becomes manifest when consciousness remembers its divine nature.

The key word here is remembrance.

We can direct our consciousness in many directions, and, in our fast paced world we can be filled with busyness and patterns of thought we are often unaware of. In order to 'remember' our true identity, our divine nature, we need to understand the fourth principle.

In opening this Fourth Universal Principle, "The Essence of Identity is Embedded in Cellular Memory", we are reminded that the Universal Intelligence has evolved life from light.

In this evolution, intelligence is imbedded into the cellular seeds that continue to inform that particular form of life of its nature and its identity, so that it can manifest itself to its fullness and potential. This principal is true for human life as well.

Our true identity as a manifestation of spirit life energy of the Universe, is embedded in our soul, which is of Divine Source..

Remembrance of this Divine nature is our true identity that is still evolving.

The I AM enables this remembrance to come forth in all the diverse experiences of our ongoing story.

The practice of Remembering Sacred Path is opening remembrance to assist us in recalling our true purpose in this life.

It is like touching into the source again and again and each time reorienting us to walk our sacred path.

THE DARKNESS IN THE HOLY WOMB OF LIFE
CONTAINS ALL LIGHT
Physical manifestation is the divine container
in which the sacred spirit resides.

HONORING THE TEMPLE
Honor the beauty of your body temple
each day with the loving care of your spirit.
Create time for:
Cleansing and Beautifying
Spiritual Movement
Good Healthy Nourishment
Calm Restful Sleep.
Allow quiet time with your body temple
to ask what is needed for
ideal health and take time on the earth
to recharge your body energy.

Practice for Principle #5
HONORING THE TEMPLE

Physical manifestation is the divine container in which the sacred spirit resides.

All matter is filled with light, vibration, energy.

A human being's physical body is made up of cellular tissue, and each cell is composed of protons, neutrons and electrons.

Further analysis leads to fine particles, which are said to be particles of light. Scientists say that these particles of light, at further depth, are light vibrations.

All of the many forms of matter that we experience in life, including our body temple, are of the light energy of the Universe.

When we truly realize the body container is the home of the spirit, a sacred container, a temple, we begin to see what is needed to care for it.

This practice of Honoring the Temple calls us to hold a high consciousness of this body temple in the way we listen to its wisdom, in the way we care for it, in the beauty with which we maintain it, and what we allow of beauty to surround it.

This higher consciousness calls us to study the subtle nature of the body intelligence and to listen to it as an expression of the Universe.

This same consciousness calls us to become conscious of any patterns of ignoring, taking for granted, exhausting, indifference or exploitation of this sacred container.

With this practice of Honoring the Temple, it is important to assure daily time for this heightened consciousness, and to listen to the body's messages.

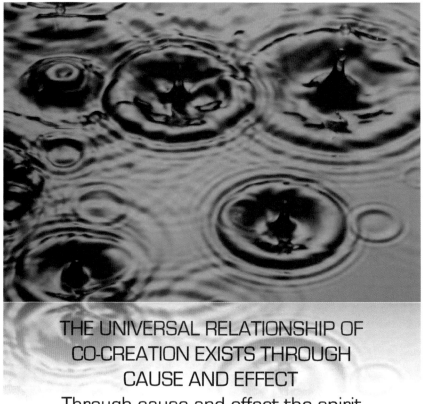

THE UNIVERSAL RELATIONSHIP OF CO-CREATION EXISTS THROUGH CAUSE AND EFFECT

Through cause and effect the spirit
consciousness co-creates the Universe.

CONSCIOUS DREAMING
From the diamond of the true self,
step on the high path of
higher consciousness,
open to all potential,
align all thoughts, words
and deeds to be life affirming.
Co-create with the spirit of the Universe.

Practice for Principle #6
CONSCIOUS DREAMING

Through cause and effect the spirit consciousness co-creates the Universe.

As we are spirit, in connection with all spirit, we are in a constant dance of the dreamweave.

Seldom does humanity realize the power of our creation, our co-creation, and therefore, is typically asleep to the universal potential inherent in this life.

When we realize that we are co-creating with the Universal Dream of Life, evolving in every moment through our thoughts, words and deeds, we are called to the responsibility of being conscious of how we affect and cause the uniqueness of our experience.

At the same time, we are called to become aware of how we affect or cause ripples in the life around us. Is the ripple we send life-affirming or life-diminishing?

As conscious dreamers we can come into the state of harmony with the Divine and consciously assist in the evolution of true peace.

The practice of Conscious Dreaming is to realize we can step on the path of higher consciousness to co-create with the Universe the kind of world and life we want.

This is indeed a practice of consciousness.

It is important to dream for ourselves, our children and our planet.

We can create the world we want to live in, and it begins with what we create in ourselves.

© Chrisbarton99 | Dreamstime.com

UNIVERSAL TRUTH INFORMS RIGHT ACTION
Right action becomes manifest when
in harmony with universal truth.

WALKING THE BEAUTY WAY
When at choice point,
listen to the spirit voice of higher truth.
Express through heart mind consciousness.
Walk the beauty way as the I AM
in every thought, word and action.

Practice for Principle #7
WALKING THE BEAUTY WAY

Right action becomes manifest when in harmony with universal truth.

When we are in connection with Universal Truth, we are accessing the source energy of the Universe.

If something is true in the universal sense, it will reflect wholeness, harmony and will be beneficial to all life.

As we act, we are in the state of creating our life. Acting in the way of the First Peace includes the thoughts, feelings, and attitudes we let take root in us, and the various forms of expression that we emit, such as sounds and body language.

To Walk the Beauty Way is a call for us to be connected with Universal Truth and to bring this consciousness into our daily life.

When we are present to this alignment, we enable this higher consciousness to guide our choices and thereby affect our outcomes in a positive way.

To develop this state of Walking the Beauty Way calls for us to bring ourselves into the I AM, often, as we listen with the heart-mind's message of what is arising in the moment.

Only if we develop this constant connection of the I AM with the heart can we be in touch with this higher consciousness of Universal Truth.

Developing our connection with the consciousness of Universal Truth is a daily practice of being in the I AM and listening to the spirit voice of higher truth.

When we encounter a choice point and connect with the heart-mind and higher truth, we will act from this truth.

Image from Hubbell Space Telescope

ALL THINGS ARE BORN OF WOMAN
Respect for the sacredness of life
enhances the life force
which emanates from the divine.

GUARDING THE SPIRIT FIRE
Stand for the sacredness of all life.
Guard your spirit fire of the First Peace.
Send the full spectrum of Love into all of life.

Practice for Principle #8
GUARDING THE SPIRIT FIRE

Respect for the sacredness of life enhances the life force which emanates from the divine.

When we accept the sacred nature of our I AM as originating from the womb of the Universe, we can begin to understand the sacredness of our life force energy and the need to tend this spirit fire.

In the self-practice of the First Peace, in Guarding the Spirit Fire in oneself, we are developing a heightened consciousness of our overall energy state of vitality and respect for our life energy as we move through the moments of our day.

If we do not tend to this fire by being conscious of the brightness or dullness of it, we can subtly diminish it by thoughts, feelings and actions that are not life-enhancing thereby disrespecting the vital life force of spirit in us.

To open this further, we see the tendency in our societies to face the challenges of low esteem, disrespect of self, undermining the natural power and gifts of each other which focus on competition, greed and overstimulation. These are all forms of disrespect of self, life, and each other. Using the practice Guarding the Spirit Fire, calls us to reverse these tendencies realizing that the fire of the spirit is essential for life to continue.

One of the best measures of being aware of the state of our own spirit fire is to be aware of our current state of happiness. Happiness is an internal state that is not dependent on an external condition, but rather our internal relationship with life and the spirit. It is characterized by a centered state of well-being regardless of external challenges we face.

Our greatest power as the human is our capacity to send the power of love into the experiences of our life and especially to ourselves. This power called "love" has many qualities, like a rainbow of different colors, with each color of "love" having a unique relevance to different conditions we meet in our experience.

Some examples of this spectrum are: compassion, quiet wisdom of presence and deep listening, the tough love of the trainer, the experienced guide, the fierce love of the good parent or healer, the dedicated teacher, the evocative leader and the guardian of the sacredness of life.

Each of these reflect a vibrant pathway to Guarding the Spirit Fire.

10 Sticks of Happiness
I am learning

See blank pg
at end.

HOW TO REGISTER AND BEGIN A FIRST PEACE CIRCLE

The Organic Structure of the First Peace Movement

All of humanity is being called to attention
by our earth planet and an evolving state
of consciousness that is shifting our collective
awareness to usher in universal peace
for the next millennia.

This is the time on our earth for the people
to come together and for us collectively
to create the world of peace
that we all dream about.

And we all know, this is only possible if we each
choose to make the changes in ourselves first.

Creating a culture of peace
that we choose to live by
is indeed a discipline.

This inner discipline we call the First Peace,
as this is the first step we must take, together.

We are each dreamers, at cause in our world.

Let us dream together.

We present the following simplified edition of the organic structure designed for sustainable and vital growth of the worldwide People's Movement of First Peace. Continue reading and discover how you might play a part.

To visualize this organic structure, imagine four concentric rings that comprise the structure.

At the center is the ring of:

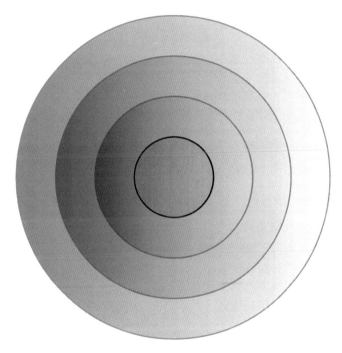

First Peace Circles
located in various communities around the world

They are at the
HEART of the MOVEMENT

The next ring out is:

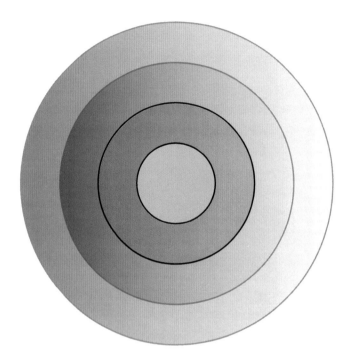

Trained Personnel

Another ring of support for First Peace Circles is a growing corps of trained
people who will provide seed planting introductions and deepening programs.

The third ring out is:

Regional & Country Cohorts

The next ring out in the organic structure
will be the development
of regional and country cohort teams
who will provide support for First Peace Circles
in their region or country.

The fourth ring out is:

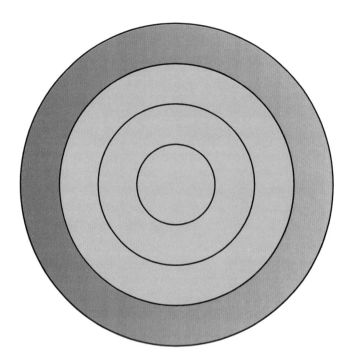

The Diamond Cohort

A council of dedicated people
who are holding and caring
for the overall movement of First Peace.

First Peace Circles

The purpose of a First Peace Circle is to create a supportive environment within a committed group of people who wish to learn and practice First Peace in order to live peace within themselves and their communities.

Following a set of Universal Principles and Practices that honor many traditions and cultures, circle members will incorporate and practice tools of higher consciousness and seek ways to carry these tools and practices into their local communities.

The primary function of a First Peace Circle is for members to create peace in their own lives and to share their learning in community thus fostering a new culture of peace and human harmony.

Activating a First Peace Circle

A Circle Leader, one who has chosen to call a group together, will act as the facilitator for the 12-month learning journey for First Peace Circle members. A curriculum of online teachings and assignments is provided including 30-minute monthly teaching segments with WindEagle and RainbowHawk available in a password-protected space viewed online.

Group discussions, teachings and individual practice are part of each monthly meeting. These meetings coupled with monthly assignments will enable all circle members to deeply integrate the principles and practices of First Peace into their lives.

Registered members of a First Peace Circle receive all needed materials including a password to the online curriculum, monthly assignments and the circle's own meeting room on the First Peace Circle online site where members connect together between monthly meetings. There will be a modest tuition fee to be shared by the circle members.

Those interested in becoming a Circle Leader are welcome to send an email to firstpeace@disciplineofpeace.org to receive the registration form and detailed information on what is needed to qualify to be a Circle Leader and how to form and guide a First Peace Circle in your community.

Finally some First Peace Circle values are important to agree on within the Circle.

We suggest this beginning list of values: listening in respect, honoring differences, speaking from the heart, keeping personal statements or feelings that have been spoken within the Circle, and maintaining clear open communication between Circle participants.

We recommend to keep open the spirit of 'the first people had questions' which will allow us to explore deeply with each other and avoid the trap of needing to have the right answer.

Each will come to resonance in themselves through exploration while this 'spirit' of openness and inquiry allows each one the space to deepen and to open.

Our Vision

First Peace Circles are sponsored by the World Foundation for the Discipline of Peace and are an outgrowth of the following vision:

International Peace Centers opens the vision to see that each of us, as light, can stand for peace, be a living center for peace, no matter where we are on the planet. As more and more individuals choose to live peace in themselves and share the energy that emanates from a peaceful center, that light will expand.

Living Peace Curriculum is based on Eight Universal Principles, which derive from the Circle of Law - an ancient earth wisdom teaching that evolved from indigenous cultures of the the Americas. These principles open the door to living peace in the self and are best opened through inquiry and practice in small groups.

Training Youth Leaders is one of the most critical and highly relevant undertakings of the World Foundation for the Discipline of Peace. Youth leaders in several different countries are already engaged with this foundation and will begin co-developing the youth training program in spring of 2009. Additionally, the World Foundation for the Discipline of Peace will develop a curriculum for schools in the Way of the Discipline of Peace.

Traditions in Collaboration calls for peoples of many traditions and cultures to come together to share practices of peace and to form supportive networks of collaborative projects within local communities. This is a way of honoring our unique ways of being and celebrating our diversity.

Councils of Peace invite us all to enter into a dialogue of what is needed to create a culture of peace on our planet. Understanding each other, gathering our collective wisdom and awakening our individual awareness are some of the deep benefits of sitting in council in our local communities. Councils can take place around a fire or around a table, enabling each of us to share the depth of what is needed to bring ourselves and our planet into a way of harmony and balance.

Background Story

The World Foundation for the Discipline of Peace is a global expression of Ehama Institute of Abiquiu, New Mexico. The Institute has been committed to a singular vision since its inception:

To mend the Sacred Hoop.

For Ehama Institute, this has meant to play our part in gathering the people around the sacred fire, to call for councils for understanding, to remember what it is to walk on the earth in balance and to live in harmony with all our relations.

Over the last 20 years in ceremonial work in many different countries, Ehama Institute has offered ancient earth wisdom teachings of the Delicate Lodge.

These teachings support the path of higher consciousness on our planet. The vision of Ehama Institute remains the same and seeks people of all traditions and cultures to collaborate in this important time.

Ehama Institute is now bringing into being the World Foundation for the Discipline of Peace, which stands for sustainable development, collaborative partnerships and living peace.

Invitation to a New Expression of Humanity

This handbook of journeying with the 8 Universal Principles is a seed that can grow in many ways in the human heart and mind.

We see that these Principles and Practices are universal and in alignment with all wisdom traditions throughout time, history and cultures from all parts of the world.

We see all of humanity is related to one universal truth, although it may be spoken in many different ways.

We see a growing number of humans joining the stream of consciousness of peace, to make the gift of life as it has been meant to be from the beginning, a celebration!

We see all of us, each in our own way, contributing to a new expression of humanity, living in peace and harmony.

If there is light in the soul,
there will be beauty in the person.
If there is beauty in the person,
there will be harmony in the house.
If there is harmony in the house,
there will be order in the nation.
If there is order in the nation,
there will be peace in the world.

Lao Tsu